DOLLHOUSES
THE COLLECTOR'S GUIDE

DOLLHOUSES
THE COLLECTOR'S GUIDE

VALERIE JACKSON DOUET

CHARTWELL
BOOKS, INC.

PAGE 1:

The splendid dollhouse made for Fanny Hayes, daughter of the President of the United States, Rutherford B. Hayes, in 1877. The original furnishings have not survived, but antique replacements have been found for the house, which is a large three-story model with an ornate central tower.

PAGE 3:

The garden room of the Sara Ploos van Amstel house in the Hague. This is a large cabinet furnished on three levels with beautifully made objects, some in gold, but many of them in silver. The dollhouse is occupied by several wax dolls, all finely dressed in fashions of the mid-eighteenth century.

BELOW:

A bedroom of the 1886 Hammond dollhouse, a 36-roomed mansion with rooms at the front and back. The rooms are a series of boxes, but service corridors run the length of the house and there are two staircases and a working elevator at one end. The house was always lit by electricity, which must have been a great innovation at the time when the house was made.

Published by
Book Sales, Inc.
114 Northfield Avenue
Raritan Center
Edison, N.J. 08818

Produced by
Brompton Books Corp.
15 Sherwood Place
Greenwich, CT 06830

ISBN 0-7858-0220-7

Printed in Slovenia

Contents

Introduction

Dollhouse collectors have always been a varied cross section of society: princes and princesses, dukes and duchesses, merchants' wives and housewives, artists and craftsmen, have all fallen under the spell of these delightful little homes in miniature, and have probably done so since the dawn of civilization.

Though doubtless played with by children, the very earliest models of houses were intended as funerary offerings; however, as long ago as the sixteenth century, it was recorded that Duke Albrecht of Bavaria had a splendid dollhouse made for his small daughter. It was a replica in miniature of the house of a German prince, four stories high with a courtyard and numerous rooms sumptuously furnished with silver and tapestries. What is not recorded is whether the duke's small daughter was actually allowed to play with it,

but it seems improbable, since when it was finished the duke put it in a museum, where it was destroyed by fire in 1674. The world of the collector and that of the child were thus oceans apart, and it was not until the nineteenth century that dollhouses became more generally regarded as children's toys.

No present-day collector could hope to find a very early dollhouse like Duke Albrecht's, or even one of the fine, large, fully furnished German houses like those in the Germanisches Nationalmuseum in Nuremberg, which were made in the early seventeenth century. From time to time, however, an early unfurnished house does surface. One such, dated 1675, appeared in a salesroom in 1988, where it fetched a huge sum of money. It was made of oak, had two floors containing two rooms on the second floor and one room on

RIGHT:
An unusual French cardboard house of the late nineteenth century, from the Musée des Arts Décoratifs, in Paris. With its high roof and large windows, it is a typical French town house of the period.

LEFT:
The kitchen of one of the houses of "Mon Plaisir," *in Arnstadt, a dolls' town of over 80 different scenes from the everyday life of an eighteenth-century German town.* "Mon Plaisir" *was created by Princess Augusta Dorothea of Schwartzburg-Arnstadt, a dedicated collector who was born in 1666. Each scene contains dolls measuring about four to five inches high, which portray royal personages, shopkeepers, entertainers and all the other great variety of people living in this imaginary town.*

the first, and it resembled a well-made closet with windows.

It might still be possible to find eighteenth-century houses, which would almost certainly be unfurnished, since it is rare to find older houses which still contain their original furnishings. Unless you are unusually wealthy or very lucky, it is best to look for houses dating from no earlier than the nineteenth century. But having said that, to the enthusiast all dollhouses are collectable, the only constraint (apart from the financial one) being that of space, for they do tend to take up rather a lot of room. Not that that deters the true collector; one such managed to fit four of them into her one-room apartment!

Although very old dollhouses are both rare and expensive, plenty of later models can still be found at auction and in antique stores, while mass-produced twentieth-century examples can be picked up for very little at rummage sales. They will probably need some restoration, but for those who like working with their hands, mending their acquisitions and making miniature furniture for them is an absorbing, if time-consuming, hobby. Such a wide range of interests is involved – including social history, interior decoration, dress fashions and architecture – that it can easily dominate your life.

It always pays to know as much as possible about your subject, and visits to museums with collections of old toys in the United States and Europe will widen your knowledge. Books will give you good background information and, for the serious collector, it is also well worth subscribing to magazines about dollhouses and miniatures, which give details about dollhouse sales and collectors' meetings, and joining local clubs, where you can exchange information and furnishing items with fellow members.

Chapter I
Early Dollhouses in Europe and the U.S.A.

Before the industrial revolution in Europe all dollhouses were made locally by craftsmen, or at home by handymen or estate workers. They seem to have been made mainly in northern Europe where, because of the cold climate, life has always been centered on the home. In southern Europe, however, in spite of the tradition of Christmas crèches, dollhouses do not appear to have been part of the culture.

A characteristic of many early baby houses (as dollhouses were called in the seventeenth and eighteenth centuries) was their resemblance to real houses, with proper exteriors and rooms connected by staircases. Certainly this is true of the seventeenth-century houses in the Germanisches Nationalmuseum in Nuremberg. These extremely detailed houses

were furnished with everything that a middle-class family and its servants needed for comfortable everyday living, and particularly remarkable are the kitchens, in which every cooking implement is a perfect miniature of the real thing. The houses were intended to teach young girls how to manage a household, and were not considered as toys but rather as display pieces, to be admired by both adults and children.

The earliest-known dollhouse in existence is a 9-foot-high house in the Germanisches Nationalmuseum in Nuremberg, which is dated 1611. The base of the house is the cellar; the first floor consists of a great hall decorated with a mural showing a picnic in a garden, and next to it is a yard with a triple gallery

OPPOSITE PAGE:
The earliest-known dollhouse in existence is the 9-foot-high house dated 1611, in the Germanisches Nationalmuseum, Nuremberg.

BELOW:
The first floor of the Nuremberg house consists of a great hall with a mural showing a picnic in a garden. Next to the hall is a courtyard with a gallery.

BELOW:
Another grand seventeenth-century dollhouse in the Germanisches Nationalmuseum, Nuremberg, is the Stromer house, dated 1639. Note the animals, living in the stable beneath the house, and the various storerooms.

which is also decorated with a lively mural. A staircase leads to the second floor, where there is a typical kitchen crammed with cooking utensils and rows of plates lining the walls on shelves. A hall leads to a living room furnished with tables, chairs and a porcelain stove. On the top floor are a bedroom with a canopied bed and a room containing ornate seventeenth-century wooden furniture and a linen press displaying a good supply of linen.

There are three other grand seventeenth-century dollhouses in the same museum,

known as the Stromer, the Baumler and the Kress houses after the families who owned them. All present a vivid picture of life as lived by a wealthy German family of that period. There are also several smaller cabinet houses in existence, such as the four-roomed example in the Bethnal Green Museum of Childhood, London, England, which has two kitchens situated side by side, along with other European houses in Strasbourg, Munich, Vienna and Basel.

Even though it does not resemble a house,

LEFT:
The Kress house, also in the Germanisches Nationalmuseum in Nuremberg, presents a vivid picture of life in a wealthy German household in the seventeenth century.

LEFT:
The kitchen of the Stromer house, showing a huge array of pewter plates and copper kitchen utensils of all kinds. One item of particular interest is the board on which household needs were marked, a sort of early shopping list for servants who could not read.

ABOVE:
The West Dean cabinet house, made in the style of the seventeenth century. There are eight furnished rooms and landings with staircases. The house was probably made in the nineteenth century, and the mixture of items in it and their varying sizes and types indicates that they were purchased separately.

one very interesting cabinet in the Nuremberg style is to be found in England at West Dean College, Sussex – a grand dwelling which was once the home of Edward James, a patron of the arts and godson of King Edward VII. This cabinet, also about 9 feet high, has a glass front which opens to reveal eight furnished rooms and central landings with staircases. The strange thing about this baby house is that it was probably made in the nineteenth century to contain items dating from the eighteenth, perhaps gathered together by some collector at about the end of the century. The mixture of items of different dates and different scales indicates that they were purchased from different places. In the kitchen there is an eighteenth-century Delft tureen, and in the linen room a nineteenth-century metal hanging birdcage. However, many of the items look as though they would be quite at home in one of the early Nuremberg houses. No one knows who ordered the cabinet to be made or who furnished it, but it may have been Edward James's mother, a woman who traveled extensively and might well have been acquainted with the original dollhouses in Nuremberg.

Seventeeth-century dollhouses are rare,

but there are a great many eighteenth-century examples in existence in different parts of Europe. Some of them are quite humble affairs – in effect a series of boxes placed in a closet. One of the most famous of these is the Ann Sharp house, which belongs to the Bulwer Long family of Norfolk, England, who have preserved it more or less as it was when it was given by Queen Anne to her god-daughter, Ann Sharp, the daughter of the Archbishop of York, in around the beginning of the eighteenth century. It was intended as a child's plaything, not as a display piece, and it is occupied by a complete household of ser-

vants and family, all of whom have been labeled with their names and titles in a neat handwriting that may have been Ann Sharp's own. There are the servants: "Sarah Gill, ye child's maid," "Fanny Long, ye chamber-maid," "Roger, ye butler," and "Mrs. Hannah, ye housekeeper"; while "Lord Rochett," "Lady Rochett" and "William Rochett, ye heir" are the family. There are some visitors as well, all of whom also have their names pinned to their clothing.

The house is quite large, standing at 5 feet 9 inches high, with nine rooms and an attic filled with miniatures. The servants' rooms

ABOVE:
The kitchen of the West Dean house is much in the style of the old Nuremberg houses, and is filled with an assortment of pots and pans and a central cooking stove covered by a canopy. The collection of pewter plates and mugs is particularly good, and there are plenty of interesting cooking implements.

RIGHT:
The oldest-known furnished dollhouse in England is the Ann Sharp house, which has belonged to the same family since the beginning of the eighteenth century. It is occupied by a household of servants and family, all of whom have been labeled with their names and titles. The great hall on the second floor is furnished as a dining room, out of which rises a staircase which does not connect with the upper floor. The lady of the house is seen descending the stairs to greet her guests.

RIGHT:
The Ann Sharp house is quite large, standing at 5 feet 9 inches high, with nine rooms and an attic filled with miniatures. The servants' rooms are on the first floor, where the housekeeper, Mrs. Hannah, has her own room. On the second floor are a kitchen, the great hall and a salon. On the upper floor are two bedrooms and a boudoir. Simple though it is, the dollhouse gives us a glimpse of family life of that period.

are on the first floor (Mrs. Hannah has a very cozy little room of her own), and on the second floor there is a kitchen, a great hall for dining, out of which rises a staircase which does not connect with the upper floor, and a salon. There are two bedrooms and also a boudoir containing a strange wax portrait of Mother Shipton, a fifteenth-century English witch. Another odd thing about this house, which was, after all, a gift from the Queen of England, is the roughness of its construction.

Some smaller English eighteenth-century dollhouses were much more sturdily made, often of unpainted oak or mahogany, with carrying handles which enabled them to travel in a coach with their young owners. Sometimes they had a staircase which would

lift out, thus making it a useful place in which to conceal the family jewels and money from highwaymen while traveling.

We can see from eighteenth-century paintings that plenty of small, homemade dollhouses were made to amuse children, but it is the grand, architect-designed houses that have survived the years, and there are several of these still to be seen in England. Big and heavy, there is no doubt that many of them were copied from real houses. The exteriors were skillfully carved to resemble brickwork and rusticated masonry, and there was a great deal of detail contained in the wooden staircases, the glazed windows, the architraves, the doors and so on. Inside the fairly low rooms were steel or brass fire grates, niches

ABOVE:
The exterior of the Manwaring house, dated 1788. This house was based on the Manwaring family home in Farnham, Surrey. The unpainted oak house lacks its original furniture but is a beautiful example of a craftsman-made dollhouse, with plenty of architectural detail. The front door does not open and there is no access to the top floor.

for ornaments, kitchen ranges with spits, and all the many other appurtenances of gracious and comfortable living, as well as plenty of fine furniture.

The Nostell Priory baby house is a perfect example of this grand style. It was commissioned in 1735 by Sir Rowland Winn and was designed by his architect, James Paine, who based it on the real Nostell Priory in West Yorkshire, England. With its unpainted wooden façade, it is displayed in a rather dark downstairs corridor, but it is lit to enable viewers to admire the beautifully carved molding and paneling in the rooms, and the perfect miniature furniture, said to have been made by the young Thomas Chippendale when he lived at nearby Otley. There is a household of servants, made of wood, and a family, whose members are made of wax, as was the convention then. The house was furnished by Lady Winn and her sister, and it was clearly not intended as a child's plaything. The parlor contains Chippendale-style chairs, brightly colored Chinese wallpaper and a very lovely writing desk. The floors are mostly uncarpeted, as would have been the custom then. The kitchen is quite small for a house of this size, but it contains a spit rack with the spits in position, a large fireplace, a dresser stocked with silver plates, and a chopping block. A doll chef stands with his knife at the ready to attack a small mouse scuttling across the floor. Another very splendid room is the yellow drawing room – one of the few in the house to boast a carpet. The architectural detail in this room, from the marble mantel to the carved cornices and the brass locks on the doors, is superb.

Uppark is another fine eighteenth-century English baby house in the grand style. It was brought to its new home, Uppark, Sussex, by Sarah Lethieullier when she went there as the bride of Sir Matthew Fetherstonhaugh in 1747, although it was possibly made a little earlier than this. The house is 4 feet 9 inches high, and stands on a 2-foot 4-inch base, making it another large example of its kind. As it has been left unaltered, apart from some exterior repainting, it represents a time capsule of life in a great country house 250 years ago. The three rooms on each floor all open individually from the front, revealing four bedrooms, a magnificent dining room with its table laid with silver and glass and including servants to wait table, a drawing room and, in the basement, a kitchen, a servants' hall and a housekeeper's room. Oak was used for the furniture on the basement floor, walnut for the middle floor, and ivory for the top floor.

Other eighteenth-century English baby houses of note are the famous Tate house, now in the Bethnal Green Museum of Childhood, which was based on a Dorset house of 1760, though "refurbished" in the nineteenth century; the Blackett house in the Museum of London, dating from 1740, with its original doll inhabitants; the baby house at Strangers' Hall, Norwich; and the Yarburgh house, a solid construction made in 1715 for the children of that family, now in the Castle Museum, York. This last house is nicely furnished and has a kitchen with an arched brick fireplace, rather like that at Nostell Priory. As the architect Vanbrugh, who was working at the nearby Castle Howard, married Henrietta Yarburgh in 1719, it is thought likely that he might have designed and possibly supervised the building of this baby house for his wife's sisters.

ABOVE:
One of the elegant bedrooms of Uppark, with a mother and two babies, one of which probably belongs to the wet nurse.

LEFT:
The Yarburgh house from Heslington Hall, Yorkshire, dated 1715. It has connections with the famous architect, Vanbrugh.

OPPOSITE PAGE, TOP:
The Nostell Priory dollhouse is a perfect example of the grand style of the eighteenth century. It was based on the real Nostell Priory in West Yorkshire.

OPPOSITE PAGE, BOTTOM:
Uppark, dated 1747, is completely unaltered since that time. It has three rooms on each of its three floors, all of which open individually.

RIGHT:
The King's Lynn baby house. This room, restored in 1984, represents the merchant's counting (book-keeping) house, hence the high desk. The merchant, a Mr. Flierden, was a Quaker, so the house is furnished in the austere style which would have been suited to his beliefs.

BELOW:
The King's Lynn baby house was designed as a replica of the home of a Dutch merchant who lived at 27 King Street, King's Lynn, Norfolk.

The King's Lynn baby house also deserves attention. Not all old houses survive intact, and this one was only discovered quite recently. Designed as a replica of 27 King Street, King's Lynn, Norfolk, in England, once the home of a Dutch merchant named Flierden, the baby house was made for his only child, Ann. Mr. Flierden set up a counting (book-keeping) house at 27 King Street, which is now the home of the King's Lynn Social History Museum, and this is where the house now rests. Before this, in the 1920s, it had been given to a Torquay children's home run by the Children's Society, which in 1984 initiated the restoration of the house. The work was carried out by Vivien Greene and a group of craftsmen who furnished the two bedrooms, dining room, music room, kitchen and counting house with modern furniture in a style suitable to the period and in accordance with the Flierdens' Quaker beliefs.

Vivien Greene's own collection at the Rotunda, near Oxford, England, includes several fine examples of eighteenth-century English baby houses. Among them are some early, unpainted traveling houses: "Portobello Road" (1700-10), which arrived with a chest containing scraps of gowns worn by Queen Charlotte and Queen Victoria; "The Dower House," with four rooms and side

windows giving light to the interior; and "Cane End House" (1756), a replica of the Vanderstegen family house, near Reading. Cane End House boasts an original winding staircase linking three floors. It was designed in the Chippendale workshops and Chippendale himself copied the furniture which he had made for the family in miniature for the dollhouse. Unfortunately, as far as we know, this no longer exists.

Longleat House, the seat of Lord Bath, possesses a very pretty dollhouse made for Lady Charlotte Thynne (afterward Duchess of Buccleuch and Queensbury) by the estate carpenter in about 1811. This has a fine library whose bookcases are filled with little books, several bedrooms, a grand central staircase to the top floor, one room furnished entirely with ivory furniture, and a very small kitchen.

There was a great deal of activity in the dollhouse world on mainland Europe in the seventeenth and early eighteenth centuries. The Netherlands in particular was a very prosperous country at that time, its ports filled with merchant ships coming from and going to countries all over the world, and the Dutch dollhouses accordingly reflect this prosperity, giving us a vivid picture of everyday life as it was lived in the houses of the wealthy middle classes. The Dutch baby

houses of this period made no attempt to recreate real houses, but instead consisted of a series of boxes set inside a cabinet and filled with a profusion of miniature furniture, silver, porcelain and ivory. They were the hobby of wealthy Dutch ladies, who commissioned craftsmen and artists to carry out their designs, which were then proudly shown to their friends. Such cabinets can still be seen in museums in Amsterdam, The Hague, Haarlem and Utrecht.

The de la Court cabinet house in the Centraal Museum in Utrecht, for example, shows us different scenes in amazing detail, such as a mother entertaining a visitor in a lying-in room while the wet nurse waits to feed the new baby; a fashionably dressed gathering playing cards for money in the music or reception room; a garden; a toy-filled nursery; a storeroom in which a maid is walking toward an egg rack; a bedroom with a silk carpet and painted ceiling; a masculine-looking room filled with pictures and works of art; a laundry room; a counting house in which the master is sitting among his papers; and a kitchen where food is being prepared.

Other splendid early Dutch cabinet houses can be seen in the Rijksmuseum, Amsterdam (the Petronella Oortman and the Dunois houses, for example), in the Gemeente-

museum, The Hague (the Sara Ploos van Amstel house), and the Frans Halsmuseum, Haarlem (the superb Blaaw house).

Sara Ploos van Amstel was the wife of a wealthy merchant, and so could afford to indulge her passion for baby houses. She acquired three old doll cabinets at auction in 1743 and took rooms from these to place in a large cabinet (now in the Gemeentemuseum, The Hague), which is furnished on three levels. Like the de la Court house, it has a garden room, a kitchen, a lying-in room, a music room, a collector's room and a nursery, but in addition it also has a porcelain room containing pieces of opaque glass painted to look like the exquisite Chinese blue-and-white porcelain which was so popular in houses of the period.

The Blaaw house also once belonged to Sara Ploos van Amstel. It has a fine exterior with many-paned windows, thus making the big step from cabinet to a realistic representation of a house. The Blaaw house contains 12 rooms, including hallways, on four floors, and is filled with the most exquisite miniatures. As well as the usual rooms, there is also the study of Dr. Ludeman (an astrologer and physician), and the porcelain room is replaced by a sumptuous silver room containing silver trays, coffeepots, porringers, candlesticks and so on, all made by renowned Dutch silversmiths and displayed in a recess at the rear of the room. The floors were painted by the artist Buttener, who did so much work on the earlier house in The Hague, while Jacob de Wit painted the ceilings.

There are also some charming, smaller cabinet houses in the Simon van Gijn Museum in Dordrecht, The Netherlands, and the Strong Museum in New York also has an eighteenth-century Dutch dollhouse.

Germany had been first to create large dollhouses, yet there are few eighteenth-century examples in the museums. One Teutonic, although Austrian, exception is an unusual model in the Vienna City Historical Museum, known as "The House of Whims," which is a copy of a folly ordered by Empress Maria Ludovica, third wife of Franz I of Austria, for the park of a private estate south of Vienna. Nothing remains of the strange house itself, but the scale model made in 1799 by Ignaz Witzmann and the painter Johann Zugner to the architect's specifications, has some remarkable murals, and although it contains no furniture, there is at least a kitchen range.

There is also a remarkable miniature creation to be seen at the Castle Museum, Arnstadt, Germany, in the form of a well-populated dolls' town called "*Mon Plaisir.*" It was the brainchild of Princess Augusta Dorothea of Schwartzburg-Arnstadt, a dedicated collector who was born in 1666. In "*Mon Plaisir*" there are over 80 different scenes arranged in glass-fronted boxes, each scene containing dolls measuring about four or five inches high. The whole life of an eighteenth-century town is portrayed in these boxes in

ABOVE:
The astrologer's room of the magnificent Blaaw house in Haarlem. The study of Dr. Ludeman contains interesting items in miniature, such as a tray holding two silver insects pulling a tiny silver coach, a box of medicine bottles, and Dr. Ludeman himself.

OPPOSITE, TOP:
The porcelain room of the van Amstel house, The Hague, containing opaque glass painted to look like china.

OPPOSITE PAGE, BOTTOM:
The cabinet baby house of Sara Ploos van Amstel is beautifully furnished and on three levels.

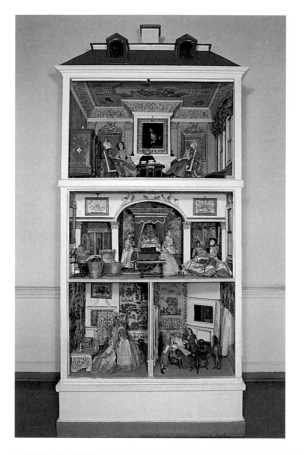

One of the dollhouses at "Mon Plaisir," a dolls' town of over 80 different scenes arranged in glass-fronted boxes, each scene containing dolls. The whole life of an eighteenth-century town is portrayed in these boxes. Here we have aristocratic people living their gracious lives in luxurious surroundings.

great detail, so that it resembles a theatrical event, the dolls acting the parts of royal personages, servants, shopkeepers, entertainers, nuns, clowns – in fact, imitating all human life. The little rooms and shops are beautifully made, and it is not surprising to learn that the princess went deeply into debt to pay for the materials and craftsmen for her hobby.

The Russians were no less keen on miniature houses during the early part of the nineteenth century, as we know from "The Little House of Nachtchokine." Nachtchokine, a friend of the writer Pushkin, began in 1830 to recreate his own home in miniature, filling it with items made by artists and craftsmen. There is a grand piano, which cost the huge sum of 1500 rubles, a dining table with hand-turned legs, bronze candlesticks and clocks, and five samovars – four of silver and one of gold. Nachtchokine fell on hard times and had to sell his dollhouse in 1840; sadly, many of the items were lost, but now that the house is displayed in the Pushkin Museum in St. Petersburg, the remaining 300 miniatures are at least safe.

The prince and princess, dressed in yellow, receive a courtier, in red, in their salon. This is another scene from life at "Mon Plaisir," Arnstadt, Germany.

The Scandinavian countries were also enthusiastic about dollhouses during this early period. The Nordiska Museet in Stockholm, Sweden, has about 30 dollhouses in its collection, among them a tall, late seventeenth-century manor house on three floors, each one of which opens separately to reveal a storeroom, a hall, and an interesting kitchen with a low cooking range. Unusually, this house actually looks like a real house, but the museum also has a very nice eighteenth-century one in a glass-fronted cabinet, furnished on four levels, one of which is occupied by an elegant ballroom with painted walls.

The Nationalmuseet in Copenhagen owns a late eighteenth-century wooden two-story house with a mansard roof which opens to reveal two rooms. It does not contain much furniture – just a bed and some chairs on the top floor, and a closet, shelves and a few chairs on the bottom – even in a prosperous merchant's house, the furnishings would have been simple at that time. This same museum also has a fine Copenhagen kitchen of about the same period: one tall room containing shelves with large cooking implements and a hooded stove, which might well have been used as a teaching aid.

The Vestlandkse Kunstindustrimuseum in Bergen, Norway, has a charming eighteenth-

A charming eighteenth-century cabinet house from Bergen, Norway, with four unusually placed rooms. Downstairs is a well-equipped kitchen and bedroom, and upstairs are two parlors.

The 1893 Uihlein dollhouse in Milwaukee, made for the daughter of the Vogel family, who became Mrs. Uihlein. Milwaukee had a large German population and this house shows the German influence, with its ornamented cupboard façade and the heads of muses on the exterior cornices.

century cabinet house, while the Finnish National Museum in Helsinki possesses several dollhouses, the earliest of which is dated 1830.

Dollhouses and toys were exported from Europe to America in the eighteenth century, but some were also certainly made there, as can be seen from the only surviving example of an early American dollhouse in the Van Cortlandt Museum in New York. This large model, made for a member of the Homans family and dated 1744, shows the influence of Dutch architecture in its realistic exterior, although the interior itself does not owe anything to any contemporary European influence. The house is arranged on two floors, containing two rooms each, those at the top being divided by wooden railings which admit light to the room at the back. Windows are painted on the outside of the house, which sits on top of a drawer holding toys and spare furniture for the house.

As there was no mass production of dollhouses in the U.S.A. in the first part of the nineteenth century, the few examples from this period are all handmade. One such is the Shelton Taylor house of 1835, in the Museum of the City of New York, where the Biedermeier interiors are lit to display their lovely colors. This museum also possesses the Brett house (1835-40), built by the Reverend Philip Milledoler Brett; and the Goelet house, made in 1845, and modeled after the residence of Peter and Jean B. Goelet on Broadway at 19th Street, which was built for their nieces by the family carpenter.

The Essex Institute, Salem, Massachusetts, has several dollhouses, among them the famous Warren house (1893), made by Israel Fellows, a Salem cabinetmaker, for the four daughters of Mrs. Annie Crowninshield War-

ren. It is elaborately furnished and is a perfect miniature picture of a mid-nineteenth-century American merchant's town house.

A further charming example is the Uihlein house (1893), which can be seen in the Milwaukee Public Museum in Wisconsin. This is a wooden house which was made for Mrs. Joseph E. Uihlein Sr. when she was a child – a present from her parents.

LEFT:
The living room of the Brett house, in the Museum of the City of New York. This house was built by the Reverend Philip Milledoler Brett from 1835-40. The doll family is obviously celebrating Christmas.

LEFT:
The Shelton Taylor house, dated 1835, in the Museum of the City of New York, with its interesting arched rooms and its Biedermeier interiors.

Chapter II
Mid- and Late Nineteenth-Century Dollhouses in Europe

By the middle of the nineteenth century, large collectors' baby houses were a thing of the past, and dollhouses had become children's playthings. Craftsmen no longer made well-proportioned rooms or staircases, but constructed basic houses with four rooms containing little in the way of architectural detail.

There were some small houses, as we can see in various paintings and book illustrations, but the poorer children's houses have rarely survived, and what we see today are the larger, more strongly made and better-preserved toys which were once to be found in nurseries and which have often been handed down through the family.

Mass production meant that toys were cheaper to buy, so more parents were able to afford them, and this is one reason why there are so many more later Victorian dollhouses available to collectors than earlier ones. There had also been a change of attitude toward children. Parents were more concerned about their education and upbringing than they had been in the past and, thanks to the efforts of educationalists, it was realized that children could learn from their toys. What better way to teach a child (and particularly a girl child) about everyday life and running a home than to give it a dollhouse?

Nineteenth-century dollhouses give us a clear idea of the life of the prosperous middle classes of that era. Their nurseries are filled with toys, their kitchens are well appointed, their bedrooms comfortable, and their living rooms filled with the fashionable clutter now eagerly sought after in antique markets. The houses are often peopled with large families and a plentiful supply of servants. German dollhouse furniture can be seen in many of the houses, for Germany had a long tradition of toymaking and exported its miniatures in large quantities all over the world. There was metal filigree furniture from Diessen, glassware and pottery from Thuringia, tin furniture from Nuremberg, ivory, bone and wood carvings from Berchtesgaden, and wooden furniture from Waltershausen.

Germany, so famous for its seventeenth-century dollhouses, made some mass-produced ones in the latter part of the nineteenth century, which can be seen in German museums and in various private collections in Europe. As manufactured by Christian Hacker, the French-looking model with a mansard roof appears again and again in slightly different forms. The roof often lifts off for access to attic bedrooms, and a staircase runs up the center of the house and stops at the second floor. A nice example is in the toy museum in Nuremberg. Dated 1870, it has a kitchen, staircase and bedroom on the first floor, and a living room and parlor on the second floor, both containing Waltershausen furniture which is distinguished by its dark wood and gold decoration.

Another typical Hacker house of about this period has an attic room set into the roof and wooden balconies both upstairs and down, forming two verandas. Christian Hacker did some market research in England when he was exploring outlets for his dollhouses and he copied houses in south London. His trademark is the initials "C.H." intertwined in a shield, with a small crown on top.

The firm of Moritz Gottschalk of Marienburg made the famous "blue roof" and later "red roof" houses based on pretty German villas, some with windows and doors printed on them, others with apertures, and most with carved wooden balconies.

The invention of lithography early in the nineteenth century meant that toys, and especially dollhouses and dollhouse furniture, could be brightened up with colored papers printed with different designs, a discovery which the German manufacturers in particular seized upon as an extra selling point. By the end of the nineteenth century, many different designs were being produced in this way by Moritz Gottschalk, including imitation brick and stone, printed beams and colorful doors and windows.

Although rooms rather than houses were popular in Germany at this time (perhaps

because many Germans, like the French, lived in apartments rather than houses, where there would have been little space for large toys), there are good examples of handmade German dollhouses of this period in Kommern and Sonneberg. One in Munich, known as Zintl's house, is made as a large fabric store, its rooms filled with bales of fabric neatly stacked on shelves, long counters, and row upon row of little jackets, hats and undergarments.

There is one type of late nineteenth-century French dollhouse which appears repeatedly in collections. Known as the "Deauville" house, it stands on a base and, like the German houses, has balconies and litho-graphed decoration. Actually, many of these so-called "Deauville" houses are so similar in style to the German ones, even possessing identical fretwork balconies, that it seems very likely that they were all made by the same German firm of Moritz Gottschalk. This small type of house was being manufactured well into the twentieth century.

There are several dollhouses in the Musée des Arts Décoratifs in Paris, some of them similar in type to the Gottschalk and Hacker ones, others handmade and based on typically French houses. One has arched windows (those on the first floor being protected by bars), a pedimented front door, a decorated cornice, and a stone-effect façade – in fact, a

OPPOSITE PAGE:
These "Deauville" houses from the late nineteenth century often appear in collections. They are quite small, usually with a balcony, and with lithographed bricks.

BELOW:
Another fine example of a Christian Hacker dollhouse.

model of a real French house. Rooms were as popular in France as they were in Germany, and there are several examples of these in the Musée du Jouet at Poissy.

The Historisches Museum in Basel, Switzerland, boasts a very fine handmade dollhouse of the mid-nineteenth century, made by an artist, Ludwig Kelterborn, for his three daughters. In the old cabinet shape, it has five floors with a staircase running through the center, and it also has front balconies. The attic holds a laundry and storage room, there are six domestic rooms, and a

basement containing stores; a wonderful plaything for three girls and in remarkably good condition after all these years.

Scandinavian countries produced some delightful dollhouses in the nineteenth century, many of which can be seen in their museums. They are often furnished with German furniture. The Legoland collection in Denmark purchased the Estrid Faurholt dolls and dollhouses, among which are Mrs. Faurholt's childhood house and "Carlsro," dated 1870-75, which has seven rooms, a hall and a toilet – the latter unusual in a Victorian

LEFT:
The "Grandmother's dolls' house" in Legoland, Denmark. Dated 1870, this is one of several dollhouses which Legoland purchased from the late Estrid Faurholt in 1966. There is no staircase, but the downstairs and upstairs rooms, all furnished in Danish style, are connected by doors.

BELOW:
The "Three Sisters" house in Copenhagen dates from about 1850. It was originally owned by the Danish royal family, and it has the cipher of Crown Prince Frederik VIII on the top. It was probably the plaything of Princesses Ingeborg, Thyra and Dagmar in the 1880s, and it is filled with interesting miniatures.

dollhouse. The sitting room is particularly fine, with a huge copper stove in one corner, a German Waltershausen writing desk, and an embroidered fire screen.

The Nationalmuseet in Copenhagen has more than 20 dollhouses, several of which date from the late nineteenth century. The "Three Sisters" house has an interesting history. Dating from 1850, it was originally owned by the Danish royal family, and has the cipher of Crown Prince Frederik VIII on its top. It was probably played with in the 1880s by Princesses Ingeborg, Thyra and Dagmar. A glass-fronted cabinet house furnished on three floors, it contains miniature sculptures and pictures of known people. The stove in the sitting room, the pictures, and the oven in the kitchen, all help to date the house.

The Villa Olga, a tall, narrow dollhouse dated 1884, has 10 windows on the front, a

RIGHT:
The Villa Olga, another Danish dollhouse, dated 1884, is about 7 feet high, and the furniture is larger than the usual inch-to-a-foot scale. The three rooms and basement are arranged as a bedroom, parlor, kitchen and storage area.

BELOW:
The dining room and the kitchen of the Hallberg dollhouse, in Helsinki. Although it is dated 1890, it is in the old cabinet style, and contains only four rooms. Because the rooms are tall, the furniture seems to be crowded into the bottom half, but there is plenty of it and it is well made.

well-equipped kitchen, a crowded sitting room and a bedroom on each of the three floors, as well as a basement and an attic. It was built by a leading furniture-maker, C. B. Hansen of Copenhagen, for 11-year-old Olga Josephsen, presumably for her birthday.

In Finland, the Museovirasto, Helsinki, has several dollhouses, the oldest of which is dated 1830. The Hallberg house, dated 1890, is a cabinet construction containing four tall rooms, in which the furniture seems to be crowded into the bottom half.

The Nordiska Museet in Sweden also possesses a number of dollhouses, decorated in what could be called "Scandinavian Victorian" style, but there do not appear to have been any mass-produced Scandinavian

houses until the twentieth century. Doubtless before this they imported them from Germany like everyone else.

In England at this time, dollhouses were an essential item in most nurseries, and a great many of them have survived and can be seen in different museums, as well as in private collections. Even Queen Victoria had one as a child (a flat-fronted, two-roomed house with a papered brick façade), and Queen Mary, as Princess of Teck, had a very ordinary six-roomed house (which is now in the Museum of London), furnished with commercially made furniture.

There is a great difference in quality between the late-Victorian English craftsman-made houses, and those which were mass-produced. Mass-produced houses were made of thin wood which often cracked underneath the wallpaper, thus splitting it. Early commercially made English dollhouses were often nothing more than a set of four boxes with a flat roof behind a fairly convincing house front. The proportions of the rooms were tall and narrow, making it quite difficult to furnish them realistically. These houses were made in London workshops, and in his book *The Cricket on the Hearth* Charles Dickens describes one such workshop in which Caleb made his dollhouses:

Caleb and his daughters were at work together in their usual working room . . . and a strange place it was. There were houses in it, finished and unfinished, for dolls of all stations in life. Suburban tenements for dolls of moderate means; kitchens and single apartments for dolls of the lower classes; capital town residencies for dolls of high estate. Some of these establishments were already furnished according to estimate, with a view to the convenience of dolls of limited income; others could be filled on the most expensive scale, at a moment's notice, from whole shelves of chairs and tables, sofas, bedsteads and upholstery.

The firm of G. & J. Lines of London produced many dollhouses during the latter part of the nineteenth century. They ranged from cheap models to those costing ten times as much, the more expensive models having a staircase. The best known of the early Lines dollhouses is the flat-fronted house with six windows and a sunburst ornament on a front door which does not open. The façade is papered with brick-and-stone-effect paper, and it opens to reveal four narrow, high rooms with chimney breasts.

Some of the least expensive mass-produced houses were made of paper, designed to be

ABOVE:
The six-roomed dollhouse which once belonged to Queen Mary of England when she was Princess of Teck. A bedroom and a nursery occupy the top floor; in the middle are a parlor and a music room; on the first floor are the dining room and a fairly humble kitchen.

packed away when not in use, which must have been a selling point for the many families living in small houses. In 1889 the English Toy Company was selling "an elegant detached villa, tastefully furnished and with all kinds of necessaries and luxuries" for Miss

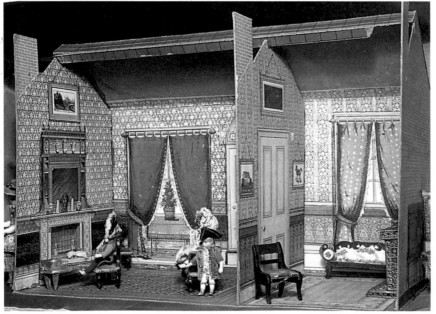

Dolly Daisy Dimple. It had:

imitation Red Brick and Stone Facings, Bay Windows, Green Venetian Blinds, Bright Colours &c. A practical two roomed house to put furniture in. The interior decorations are all in the modern style. Dados, Bright Wallpapers &c. Can be taken to pieces and packed flat for transit or storage and can be rebuilt in a few seconds . . . It is quite a large Doll's House and takes the place of a Doll's House usually costing ten times the money. Price ONE SHILLING complete.

There is no shortage of later nineteenth-century handmade English dollhouses to study, both in museums and in private collections, and more are always coming to light. There are so many, in fact, that it would take an encyclopedia to list them all, but a good place to start is at the Bethnal Green Museum of Childhood in London, which has several notable ones in its collection. One grand house, called "Mrs. Bryant's Pleasure," is a plain, flat-fronted house with a balustrade along the top, which was made for a Mrs. Bryant of Oakenshaw, Surbiton, England, in the 1860s. Mrs. Bryant was clearly interested in interior decoration, as the house is full of rather large but beautifully made furniture, the armchairs properly upholstered, the drapes made by Mrs. Bryant herself.

"Dingley Hall' is another house at Bethnal Green, and it was made in 1874. An unusual fact about this house is that it was made for two boys, Isaac and Laurence Currie, who obviously took great pride in furnishing it. Laurence was 14 years old when the house was made, and he had been collecting miniatures since he was a small child. He added to his collection all his life, picking up items on his travels abroad and bringing them home to add to the house, which is large and very masculine in style, filled with male dolls, weapons, shields holding trophies, and a wall-mounted stag's head. Also to be found at Bethnal Green is "Miss Miles's house," made by Miss Amy Miles in the 1890s. This was probably a

TOP LEFT:
A flat-fronted, box-back dollhouse, of the type made in England toward the end of the nineteenth century by the firm of G. & J. Lines.

LEFT:
A rare English Toy Company cardboard house of 1889. Designed for "Miss Dolly Daisy Dimple," it had two rooms printed with colorful interior decorations.

commercially made house, with a side wing added on later. Old photographs show that a ladder once led from a storage room on the top floor to a penthouse studio.

Wallington Hall in Northumberland is a large country house owned by the National Trust (the British national conservation organization), containing a collection of 15 or so dollhouses dating from 1845 to 1930. Most of the houses were presented to the National Trust in 1973, together with their contents, by the family of Mrs. Bridget Angus of Corbridge, who had collected them throughout her lifetime. The star of the collection is Hammond house, a 36-roomed mansion with rooms at the front and back, which was made in about

BELOW:
"Hartley Hall," a grand, hand-built dollhouse of imposing proportions. Dated about 1880, it has six rooms which have been lovingly restored by its new owner.

ABOVE:
The interior of Hartley Hall, showing the six rooms and central staircase, all beautifully restored and filled with suitable furniture and ornaments.

RIGHT:
The parlor of a typical dollhouse of the late nineteenth century. Note the gilt-framed pictures, the Chinese shadow box, the piano with its pleated fabric front, and the hand-made canvas-work carpet.

1886 as a special order, probably by an estate joiner. Service corridors run the length of the house and there are two staircases and a working elevator at one end. Though not a piece of great craftsmanship (the rooms are simply a series of boxes), it is interesting in many ways. For example, it was always lit by electricity, which must have been a great innovation at the time that it was made. Originally, water was piped from tanks on the roof to the bathtub in the one and only bathroom, and from there to the sink in the scullery below, a charming piece of realism which no longer exists because the pipes perished and it was impossible to replace them without damaging the decorations. Most collectors of old dollhouses are agreed that the original decorations should be preserved at all costs. There are rooms for everything and everyone: a scullery, a boot room, complete with a row of bells with which to summon the servants, a kitchen, a butler's pantry, a housekeeper's room, a nursery, several bedrooms, a dining room, parlor, and so on, along with a huge quantity of china-headed dolls representing family and staff.

"Claremont," a sturdily made three-story house dated 1867, has a painted brick façade and a small front garden with a gate. The six rooms all open separately to reveal two bedrooms, a bathroom, a living room, a dining room, and a kitchen with a brick oven, all furnished with well-made furniture in very good condition. Another six-roomed house at Wallington Hall has finer furniture in it, and someone has gone to the trouble of making *petit point* carpets throughout and also a hand-embroidered bellpull for one of the rooms. In one bedroom, "mother" is having a rest, while "father" is in the upstairs parlor reclining on a chaise longue. This house has a grand entrance hall with a hat tree in it, a wall tapestry, and a dog waiting to be taken for a walk. A slightly later house goes even further in terms of grandeur, its baronial hall containing a bearskin rug and a pair of antlers on one wall. The kitchens of the older houses are all furnished with the usual kitchen range and an array of huge pots and pans.

A unique collection of dollhouses can be seen at the Rotunda, Oxford, in England, which is owned by Vivien Greene, who started to collect them after World War II when few others were interested in the subject. Among the many fine houses there, some of which date back to the eighteenth century, is the Coburg house, a beautiful mid-nineteenth-century house, so named because this was chalked on its roof when it was purchased. Nora Earnshaw describes this house in her

BELOW:
The nursery of Hammond house, a 36-roomed mansion which was made in about 1886, probably by an estate joiner. It is in Wallington Hall, Northumberland, and it arrived with all its original furniture, which is unusual for a house of this age.

ABOVE:

"Claremont" dollhouse, a robust three-story house dated 1867. It has a painted brick façade and a small front garden with a gate. The six rooms all open separately to reveal two bedrooms, a bathroom, a living room, a dining room, and a kitchen with a brick oven, all furnished with well-made items in good condition.

book *Collecting Dolls' Houses and Miniatures* (Collins, 1989):

When acquired, Coburg House was unfurnished except for two chandeliers and one picture, all dating from the 1870s. The double staircase and most of the window frames were in fragments, but the fruitwood panelling of the large ground-floor hall was intact. Layers of modern paper had to be removed and the only original paper is in the master bedroom on the first floor.

Coburg house has been furnished as if it were an English hunting box owned by one of Queen Victoria's more obscure relations . . . and this explains the number of mementoes and photographs of the Queen. The period is *c.* 1870-90. Some of the furniture is nineteenth century, and some of the pieces are modern replicas . . . The scarlet silk curtains are part of a vestment bought in the Sunday market at Brussels from a convent now closed.

The coronet on the sheets was specially embroidered. The real stained-glass window was copied from an old church in Munich and was created by Mrs. June Astbury. The stables contain horses made by "Julip"; each horse has its name on a brass plate over its manger – Teck, Balmoral, Sefton and Albany.

This description gives us a good idea of the loving care and attention to detail which Vivien Greene lavishes on all her dollhouses.

Another, slightly earlier, house in the collection is "Whiteway," which was formerly housed at Saltram House, Plymouth, England. Its owner, Lord Morley, who died in 1962, gave it to his footman for his small daughter. When the National Trust took over the real house, the dollhouse had already been sold to a local antiques dealer, who offered it to the National Trust. The National Trust refused it because it was a replica, not of Saltram but of an early house which had once belonged to the same family. However, it has now been willed back to the National Trust, which will doubtless one day restore it to its home. Vivien Greene describes the house interior in great detail in her book *Family Dolls' Houses* (G. Bell & Sons, 1973):

The original wall coverings survive except in the hall and linen room. The left-hand bedroom has some original furniture – the bed with its chintz hangings, the matching curtains, and the handmade carpet of rosebuds on a claret ground. The cast-iron hob grate in the corner is embellished with a fall of flowers and, on each side, with a head of Queen Victoria as a young woman and a crown. It was made by a local blacksmith. In the other bedroom, all the furniture except for the dressing stool is original, as is the carpet.

Other interesting rooms are the living room, a schoolroom and a library, which contains books made of carved wood – each one different – and a rare globe, dated 1851.

A later dollhouse at the Rotunda is St. Faith's Vicarage, a red-brick Gothic house consisting of 11 rooms. There is also the 1865 four-roomed Bidden house, made for the children of George Bidden, a distinguished engineer from one of whose grandchildren Vivien Greene purchased the house; and Queen Victoria's Golden Jubilee house, which is decorated with flags and bunting to celebrate the queen's 50 years on the throne in 1887. The Cedars, Woodbridge, is a Suffolk

"Red Gables" is a four-roomed house with an entrance hall and staircase, dated 1886. The style of architecture is interesting, with its arched front door and bay windows with battlemented tops. The brick exterior is painted, and the front opens in three sections for easy access.

"Gordon House" at Cockthorpe Hall Museum, Norfolk, has a fine parlor, a kitchen with a cast-iron range, and a conservatory on two floors. The house remained in the same family for years, owned by one child, who then passed it on to her daughter.

house notable for its long living room decorated with gilt pilasters and filled with furniture from 1860-90.

The Abbey House Museum, Kirkstall, Leeds, has a fine mid-nineteenth-century dollhouse named "Abbey Grange," with 10 rooms and a central staircase. One interesting room is the bathroom, containing a bath with an overhead shower, jugs and water bowls, several buckets and cans — but no toilet.

Mention must also be made of the Ribchester Museum of Childhood in Lancashire, England, which has over 50 dollhouses; and of "Gordon House" at Cockthorpe Hall Museum, Norfolk, which has a very fine parlor, a kitchen with a cast-iron range into which water can be poured, and a conservatory on two floors. The house remained in the same family for years, owned first by Beatrice Mabel Gordon, who played with it under supervision and passed it on to her daughter, a lady who was in her eighties when the house came into the possession of the museum.

Chapter III
Mid- and Late Nineteenth-Century Dollhouses in the U.S.A.

It would be impossible to write about doll-houses in the United States without referring to the work of the one person who knows more about the subject than anyone else, namely Flora Gill Jacobs.

A collector of toys and dollhouses for well over 35 years, and author of *A History of Dolls' Houses* and the more recent *Dolls' Houses in America* (1974), Mrs. Gill Jacobs opened her Washington Dolls' House and Toy Museum in 1975, dedicated to the theme of historical preservation in miniature.

She chose the title of her book *Dolls' Houses in America* with some deliberation. As she says in her preface:

Although it is now clear, after nearly three years of hard labor, that a book entitled *American Dolls' Houses* would

have been possible, the multitude of commercially made houses and the tidal wave of furniture and accessories which have come to our shores, suggest that perhaps it is just as well such a work was not attempted.

In fact, her book casts its net widely and includes both American classic dollhouses and those from other countries, presenting a mouth-watering selection that makes the enthusiast yearn to see at least some of them. Fortunately, there are photographs in existence that do justice to some of these craftsman-made houses of the mid- and late nineteenth century, and others that show us the commercially made examples that were being mass-produced at this time.

A fine craftsman-made house is the Bessie

OPPOSITE PAGE:
The Bessie Lincoln dollhouse, 1876, was made of unpainted wood by John W. Ayers, and was decorated for the Christmas holiday.

LEFT:
The kitchen of Horatia's house (1860), a dollhouse in the Toy and Miniature Museum of Kansas City. With a few exceptions, the furnishings are original. The house was owned by Horatia Jones, who died in 1969 at the age of 93.

filled with delightful miniatures that include a tiny umbrella stand in the front hall, a "Waltershausen" desk and other carved pieces in the parlor, and tiny books and another desk in the dining room, many of which must have been given to Bessie by those good ladies. The house is decorated for Christmas each year by the Ladies' Committee, with fir trees and holly wreaths and gifts for each member of the doll family.

The unusually named "Sanitary Fair" house, belonging to the Delaware Historical Society, at Wilmington, Delaware, was made in 1864, even though the date 1776 is painted over the door. The house was exhibited at a fair to raise money for sick and wounded Civil War soldiers. A Miss Catharine Biddle of Philadelphia had donated the model to the fair, which took subscriptions of $10 on it. It was designed by a firm of architects in an austere Italianate style and was built to these instructions by a Philadelphia carpenter.

Behind its rather plain exterior are three stories containing nine rooms (three of them at the back): a kitchen, two bedrooms, a parlor, a dining room, a library, a games room, a maids' room and, something only occasionally seen in a dollhouse, an art gallery. This displays 25 pictures in gilt frames, mainly landscapes, which were painted by several well-known artists of the day, and a nice touch is the circular ottoman in the center of the room, positioned to enable visitors to view the pictures comfortably. It is interesting to note that the suite of marble-topped faux rosewood furniture in the dining room (possibly Waltershausen) came from the shop of Charles P. Dare, a retailer of fancy goods, who must also have provided several of the other French and German pieces in the house, all of which help to recreate the mixture of styles typical of many American Victorian-period homes of the time.

ABOVE:

The "Sanitary Fair" house, made in 1864. This was exhibited at a fair to raise money for sick and wounded Civil War soldiers. Behind its austere exterior are nine rooms, three of which are at the back. An interesting feature is the art gallery, displaying 25 pictures in gilt frames.

Lincoln house at the Peabody and Essex Museum, Salem, Massachusetts. It was made of unpainted wood by John W. Ayers in 1876 for Bessie Lincoln, who presented her dollhouse to the museum in 1953 when she was 85 years old. This oak house is elaborately furnished in the revival style popular in America in the late nineteenth century. "Some of the Salem ladies joined with my mother in furnishing the house," wrote Bessie Lincoln Potter (as she became on marriage), and it is

RIGHT:

The elaborate Roth house, designed by Leonard Roth, perhaps for the Philadelphia centennial year in 1876. The house is unfurnished, but there is a double staircase inside, and there are sash windows.

The elaborate Roth house in the Smithsonian Institution, Washington, provides a complete contrast in style. Flora Gill Jacobs questions its place among dollhouses, suggesting that it is rather more an architectural model. It was designed by Leonard Roth (perhaps for the Philadelphia centennial year in 1876), who made use of metal in the gas fixtures and the roof rail, helping to give a fine finish to this very complex and detailed structure. The house is unfurnished, but there is a double staircase and there are sash windows.

Yet another delightful craftsman-made

house is to be seen in the Wenham Museum, Wenham, Massachussetts. It was made by Benjamin H. Chamberlain, a Salem silversmith and jeweler, who worked on the house from April to December 1874 as a Christmas present for his daughters, Mamie and Millie. It was built at his store, and much of the furniture in it was donated by customers who were fascinated by watching the progress of the dollhouse. Details such as a silver plaque on the front door inscribed with the words "Mamie-Millie," a silver tea set, handwrought gilded railings on the cupola, the central bay, and the kitchen wing, all add to the charm of this beautifully made house, as do the draperies with their fringed valances hanging at the bay windows, the linen and the dolls' clothes, all made by Mrs. Chamberlain.

The Hayes house, in the Rutherford B. Hayes Library, Fremont, Ohio, is yet another classic dollhouse of about the same period. Dated 1877, it was made for 10-year-old Fanny Hayes, daughter of the then president of the U.S.A., and was presented to her mother at a fundraising fair the following year. The original furniture is no longer in the house, but it has been furnished with replacement

Washington Dolls' House and Toy Museum

pieces of the right period. It is a three-story house with an attic and a staircase, bay windows and a double door.

The Washington Dolls' House and Toy Museum owned by Flora Gill Jacobs has a fine collection of dollhouses, of course, which is being added to year by year. Among them is a

ABOVE:
A mid-nineteenth-century four-roomed New Hampshire dollhouse in the Washington Dolls' House and Toy Museum. The rooms and hall are framed, so that the façade looks like a series of boxes.

LEFT:
The beautifully crafted Chamberlain dollhouse, made by a Salem silversmith of that name who worked on the house from April to December 1874 as a Christmas present for his two daughters, Mamie and Millie. Their names are inscribed on a silver plaque on the front door.

Washington Dolls' House and Toy Museum

large New England Victorian house, built to the unusual scale of one-and-a-half inches to the foot. Because of this, it has been quite difficult to furnish. All the wallpaper is original except in the kitchen, where shreds were replaced with antique-type papers sold by the museum. Only the stove and a few minor pieces are original to the house.

The mid-nineteenth-century four-roomed New Hampshire house has fine proportions and a central staircase. The rooms and halls are framed, so that looking at the façade is like looking into a series of boxes, with windows at the rear of the house to add an air of realism. It is furnished with tin and iron furniture.

Yet another impressive house in the

Washington Dolls' House and Toy Museum is the Tiffany Platt house, which was sold to Flora Gill Jacobs as having been built for the Tiffany family of New York, though there is some doubt about this. Certainly it appears to have been built for a wealthy family, and though not all the original furnishings remain, the five rooms are filled instead with the sort of little gilt knickknacks which were available in toy stores in Europe at this time, and were probably imported into the U.S.A. from Germany, where they were made.

Commercial manufacturers were producing large quantities of dollhouses by the end of the nineteenth century. The firm of Bliss had been established in 1832, and produced wooden screws and clamps for piano- and cabinetmakers. It is not known when the company started to make toys, though its first listing as such was in 1871 and by 1889 it was advertising the "Bliss Fairy Doll House," costing 50 cents. Two boxes made up the floors, and a third formed the roof unit. In 1895 Bliss included a pretty church in its catalog, which was made as a construction toy, the 9-inch-square base forming a case for the parts, which comprised a two-piece tower with a spire, three peaked roofs with gables and 11 finials, all in the brilliant lithographed colors characteristic of the firm.

This same 1895 catalog listed three folding houses, while the 1896 catalog includes an interesting trio of buildings named "Dollyville," which made up into an opera house, a bank, and a market and grocery store. From then on Bliss produced dozens of designs – suburban homes, modern city residences, warehouses, fire stations, forts, lighthouses, stables and farms – until it was taken over in 1914 by

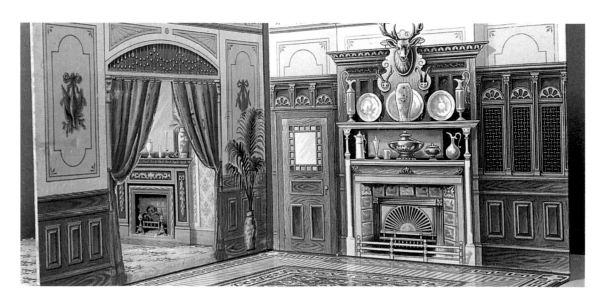

another firm, which continued to manufacture its toys for some years.

Many examples of Bliss houses are to be found in the Washington Dolls' House and Toy Museum, where Flora Gill Jacobs has created a "Bliss Street" to show them off to their best advantage. It also contains houses by the firms of McLoughlin and Converse (whose history is described fully in Chapter IV), and by Stirn and Lyon, a firm which patented in 1881 a knockdown house with a mansard roof, dormers and a balcony, as well as a lithograph-on-wood house with a lid that folded down to form a garden.

There are dozens of museums across the United States with dollhouses, old and new, in their collections, so many that it would probably take a year to visit them all. However, the visitor could, with careful planning, take in some of the following.

A good place to start is the Strong Museum in Rochester, New York, which was formerly the Margaret Woodbury Strong Museum, founded by that lady in 1937. Mrs. Strong came from a wealthy family and traveled a great deal with her parents when she was a child. When she grew up and married, she became a formidable collector of decorative items, household tools and textiles, books, paper ephemera and "playthings," which she kept in her large mansion in Rochester, New York, and which was known as the Margaret Woodbury Strong Museum of Fascination. After the early death of her husband and child, Mrs. Strong devoted the rest of her life to collecting until, at her death, she had amassed the amazing total of 27,000 dolls and 400 dollhouses, as well as room settings, stores and kitchens, all of which are now in the care of the Strong Museum.

The Museum of the City of New York, which was founded in 1923 and opened to the public in 1932, has a smaller collection of 12 historic dollhouses and many miniatures. The museum was refurbished in 1984 to show to better advantage the Brett, the Shelton Taylor, the Elder, the Stettheimer, and all the other famous dollhouses it owns, as well as its other toys and miniatures. A recent addition to the collection is the *c.* 1970 palace by Evaline Ness, author and illustrator of children's books, a dollhouse which is noted for its wall, floor and ceiling needlework tapestries.

In Denver, Colorado, is the Denver Museum of Miniatures, Dolls and Toys. Among its dollhouses is the Kingscote doll-

house (see page 77), built in 1987 as an exact replica of an 1839 Newport, Rhode Island mansion. This 16-roomed house has inlaid parquet floors of oak, teak, cherry and Brazilian rosewood, 36 electrical fixtures and 54 windows. Among the exquisite furnishings in the dining room are gold flatware, handmade crystal glassware, handpainted porcelain place settings, and a silver candelabrum.

Angels Attic is a museum of dollhouses, miniatures, toys and dolls in Santa Monica, California. Founded in 1984, it has over 60 dollhouses of different sizes and styles dating from the end of the eighteenth century to date, most of them furnished. Among them are the "Steamboat Gothic" house, a German "red roof" house, and an eight-roomed Southern colonial mansion built in 1969.

The Toy and Miniature Museum of Kansas City has several dollhouses too, among them some by Jim Marcus and Bill Robertson.

house (see page 77)

LEFT:
A fascinating "Steamboat Gothic" mansion, with ornate pillared balconies and porches, elaborate cornices, and an imposing turret. This house, dated about 1870, is said to have been constructed by a one-armed Civil War veteran.

BELOW:
Toward the end of the nineteenth century, manufacturers were trying out new materials, as this metal "Watertown" house shows. It has its original furnishings, and an added kitchen wing which has a sink with faucets. The house probably dates to the 1870s.

Chapter IV
Early Twentieth-Century Dollhouses in Europe and the U.S.A.

Although there are several memorable craftsman-made dollhouses on the grand scale, by the early twentieth century manufacturers in both Europe and the United States had proliferated and were producing some interesting smaller wares, many of which are now collectors' items.

In the U.S.A. the manufacturing firms which had started up late in the previous century continued to produce their dollhouses well into the 1920s and 1930s. The firm of Schoenhut, for example, had been founded in 1872 by Albert Schoenhut, who had emigrated from Germany to Philadelphia where he first made toy pianos, circuses and dolls before turning his hand to dollhouses. These were mostly small and neat, made of wood and fiberboard, with porches, balconies and side openings so as not to alter the appearance of the house during play. Great use was made of brilliantly colored lithography on the interior walls, and interior doors were printed on the walls, half open, with a perspective view of another room beyond to give a trompe l'oeil illusion of space. Thick, embossed paper representing stone, brick or tile, was used to great effect on these houses, some of which had as many as eight rooms, but which went down in size and design to little bungalows of only one room, and apartment-house rooms which could be purchased individually and then joined together with strips of molding. Schoenhut produced houses and bungalows until 1934, when the company finally went out of business.

The firm of Rufus Bliss was established in 1832, earlier than that of Schoenhut and, as we have seen, was producing dollhouses in the 1880s. By the early 1900s, its brightly colored lithographed houses, stables, stores and cabins were found in homes all over America. They are easily recognized by their elaborate, richly decorated architectural style. Among them was a house with two stories and an attic that folded into a flat pack; a one-story house measuring only 17 inches in height; garages with brick walls and sliding doors containing automobiles; and many other designs in a huge variety of shapes – some with balconies, some without, some with porches at the front and at the side, many with gables and balustrades, isinglass windows and lace curtains, all in attractive, bright colors that must have made them irresistible to young children.

Another American firm producing dollhouses was that of Converse, which was established in 1878 to make boxes, but soon moved into dollhouses, which were lithographed directly onto the wood rather than onto a paper covering. In her book *The Collector's History of Dolls' Houses*, C. E. King describes the beginning of the firm:

> It was established by Morton E. Converse in 1878 for the manufacture of wooden strawberry and fig boxes but was diverted into simple toys after he had amused his sick daughter by making her a dolls' tea table from an old collar box . . . It served to give him inspiration for other children's toys in such number that his company eventually dominated Winchendon, Mass.

Converse dollhouses are attractive in their way, almost primitive in style and easily distinguishable from Bliss and Schoenhut dollhouses. Converse produced the wood and fiberboard "Really Truly Doll House" in 1931 which, in spite of its bow windows and elegant front door, did not succeed in saving the firm from extinction shortly afterward.

The idea of a lightweight cardboard folding house which could be put away at the end of playtime had great appeal for families living in smaller houses, and it was one which was taken up by several American manufacturers.

The firm of McLoughlin had been founded in the late nineteenth century by the printer John McLoughlin, and the influence of the printing trade is clearly seen in the company's dollhouses, which were made of cardboard and designed to be folded flat. Their "Dolly's Playhouse," which appeared between 1884 and 1903, was made of strawboard and wood

OPPOSITE PAGE, TOP:
Schoenhut dollhouses were mostly small, neat and made of wood and fiberboard. Great use was made of brightly colored lithography.

OPPOSITE PAGE, BOTTOM:
Converse dollhouses are more primitive in their style than those of Schoenhut, though at first sight they look alike.

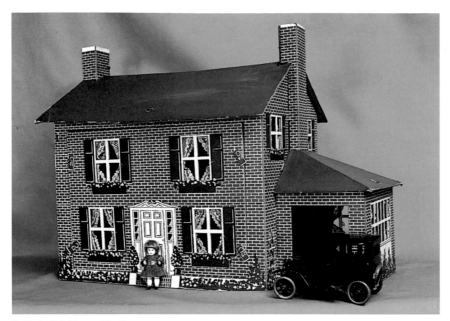

Washington Dolls' House and Toy Museum

ABOVE:

A suburban dollhouse by Dowst Manufacturing Co. of Chicago. This firm made metal dollhouse furniture, and also heavy board dollhouses and rooms in the 1920s under the name of "Tootsietoy." These houses were shipped to Britain knocked down and packed flat for easy transport.

Another delightful McLoughlin design, dated about 1911, was the "Garden House," a town house with a brick exterior punctuated by a great many windows and three doors. To make the garden and to give access, the front of the house dropped down to reveal a formal garden with a small central pool. The interior was lithographed with fireplaces with overmantels, mirrors, shelves, window seats and a parquet floor in the upstairs room.

Stirn and Lyon of New York also made folding houses, though since they were made of wood they were much heavier than those of McLoughlin and were generally not so cheerfully attractive.

Another American company, the Dowst Manufacturing Co. of Chicago, made metal dollhouse furniture and heavy board dolls' mansions and rooms in the 1920s under the name of "Tootsietoy." The company's "Modern Spanish" mansion was an impressive affair with arched windows and an ornate front door, but Dowst also made a more modest suburban design. These dollhouses were shipped to Britain knocked down and packed flat in an attractive carton.

"Tootsietoy" is a name which is easily confused with "Tynietoy," another American firm making furniture and expensive wooden dollhouses in the 1920s, although they also had a cheaper range of cottages.

There are two outstanding noncommercial

with cloth hinges, and was a sturdy folding house which needed no extra fastenings. It was a colorful two-roomed affair with three hinged walls forming the back and sides, and with an open front containing an upper bedroom with little in the way of furnishing except lithographed windows with drapes and a fireplace, and an elegant downstairs living room with a gold mirror frame, gold cornices at the windows and a bright, printed carpet. It gives us an excellent idea at the state of interior decoration at the beginning of the twentieth century.

RIGHT:

One of the outstanding noncommercial dollhouses of early twentieth-century America, the Stettheimer house, made by Carrie Stettheimer in 1923, was fashioned out of wooden packing cases. It provides us with a vivid picture of the lifestyle of a wealthy, cultured family of that time. Here, visitors are looking at the collection of pictures in the gallery of the house, all of them paintings by famous American artists of the 1920s.

American dollhouses of the early twentieth century. The first is the Stettheimer house, made by Carrie Stettheimer in 1923 out of wooden packing cases which, though not a beautifully constructed piece of work, is interesting in that it provides us with a fascinating picture of the lifestyle of a wealthy, cultured family of that time. On the left of an entrance hall decorated with a formal perspective garden, is a blue-and-white kitchen, on the right a library-cum-games room with a Chinese-type lantern, red furniture, spindly chairs and some books, one of them by Henri Waste, the pseudonym of Carrie's novelist sister. Other rooms include a linen room, a nursery, bedrooms, a butler's pantry, a parlor, a dining room and an art room containing miniature paintings by famous American artists of the 1920s.

The other outstanding early twentieth-century American dollhouse is Colleen Moore's fairy-tale castle, made by her father in 1928 in collaboration with two movie-set designers. Made in copper and aluminum, the castle is 12 feet high, with battlements, turrets and pinnacled towers. The mechanism to work the lighting and plumbing (for there is running water), is tucked away under its base.

The castle has 11 rooms filled with costly treasures, some of which were made especially for Colleen. A chandelier in the living room, for example, is made from gold and real diamonds, emeralds and pearls; the furniture in the living room is silver, while the bathroom of the princess who is supposed to be inhabiting this castle is made of crystal and jade. The dining room represents the Great Dining

ABOVE AND BELOW: Colleen Moore's fairy-tale castle. Its library (below) has nautical murals. Two arched doorways lead to the garden of Aladdin, and the bookshelves contain books of original stories.

Hall of King Arthur and his knights. Tall, shield-backed chairs surround the semi-circular table which is set with a service of gold, the forks marked with a monogram almost too small to see with the naked eye. The library contains miniature books by American authors; the garden, in which a nightingale sings, has gold and silver trees and a weeping willow that really weeps. Cinderella's silver coach, drawn by four silver horses, waits outside, and the steeple bells chime every five minutes. The castle is an amazing creation, perhaps just a little too ostentatious for today's simpler taste, but remarkable nevertheless.

In England, the firm of G. & J. Lines, which had begun to manufacture dollhouses in the previous century, became the market leader in the early to middle years of the twentieth century. George Lines had begun his career in 1870 making rocking horses, and he was joined by his brother Joseph in 1880. The first mention of dollhouses among their wares was in 1898, though they were probably making them before that date. After World War I, three of Joseph Lines's sons set up on their own to form a new company, Lines Brothers, using the name Triangtois, later abbreviated to Tri-ang. The original firm of G. & J. Lines continued in business until 1931, when Joseph died and the company merged with Tri-ang.

The brothers soon branched out from lithographed, paper-covered houses into higher quality, more expensive designs, such as the

BELOW:
A G. & J. Lines "Kits Coty" dollhouse of the early twentieth century. This was described as "a really splendid mansion, elaborately fitted up, inside and out. Staircase, doors to rooms, French windows. Curtains, beautiful papers on the walls etc. 33 inches high."

"Kits Coty" house (so called by collectors after a photograph of one of this name was shown in an early copy of *International Dolls' House News*), described as "a really splendid mansion, elaborately fitted up, inside and out. Staircase, doors to rooms, French windows. Curtains, beautiful papers on the walls etc. 33 inches high." After this they produced a huge variety of house styles, all reflecting the middle-class architecture of each decade until 1971, when they went out of business. Many of their dollhouses can still be found in auction rooms and can be identified from old catalogs.

The styles vary from the early flat-fronted houses to elaborate models with balconies and porches, from there to the "Stockbroker Tudor" of the 1920s and later, thence to Princess Elizabeth's thatched house of 1932 – a gift to her from the people of Wales – to the "modern flat-roofed suntrap" houses of the 1930s. After a break during World War II, Tri-ang went back to Tudor and Queen Anne styles in the 1950s, and to plain modern houses and bungalows in the 1960s. The company's last houses had plastic roofs (which, incidentally, did not wear very well, in spite of being advertised as "strong and resilient") and "realistic moulded windows and shutters and special sliding fronts."

There was a resurgence of interest in dollhouses in England in the 1920s and 1930s, when several firms started to make cheap flat-pack and cardboard houses, all of which are now sought after by collectors.

In 1936, Meccano Ltd. produced a dollhouse called the "Dolly Varden," designed to accompany its metal 1:24 "Dinky Toy" dollhouse furniture. As Margaret Towner writes in her book *Dolls' House Furniture* (Apple Press, 1993): "The house was of flimsy folding cardboard, and the furniture, unknown to the company, contained the seeds of its own destruction, in that the alloy used was unstable and could disintegrate in time." Perhaps it is just as well that production ceased with the outbreak of World War II, but the furniture is still prized by collectors. In Marion Osborne's *A to Z, 1914 to 1941, Dolls' Houses*, an advertisement for the Dolly Varden house and Dinky Toy furniture shows two children playing with what seems a very large Tudor-style house, but which is, in fact, only 18½ inches high. It stands on its opened-out container, forming a garden with a tennis lawn, carriage drive and rock garden. The house, made of re-inforced leather, is described as "Collapsible

and the exterior is designed to represent a half-timbered dwelling, while the interior decorations . . . printed in nine colours, are in attractive modern style." It cost nine shillings and sixpence, unfurnished.

At about the same time, "Hobbies" Limited of Dereham, Norfolk, England, which had introduced fretwork into Britain in the late 1890s, advertised a complete dollhouse kit, with furniture, which could be ordered by mail. The materials, containing a parcel of wood, glasses, mirrors, hinges, dollhouse paper etc. for making the house and 26 pieces of furniture, cost 24 shillings, collect. A book of instructions for making the house cost one shilling and sixpence. An interesting version of a house made to this Hobbies plan can be seen in Angels Attic in Santa Monica, U.S.A., proving that the firm of Hobbies traveled a long way from its native shores. Incidentally,

ABOVE, TOP:
Lines merged with Tri-ang in 1931. This typical Lines/Tri-ang "Stockbroker Tudor" dollhouse of 1932 was a very popular style which was manufactured by Tri-ang right up to the end of the 1950s.

ABOVE:
Always up-to-date with its designs, Tri-ang produced its "suntrap" houses toward the end of the 1930s. The little room on top was the sun lounge.

ABOVE:
Meccano Ltd.'s "Dolly Varden" dollhouse of 1936. Its container opened out to form a garden.

BELOW:
An Amersham house, produced in England in the late 1930s.

lapping wood-strip roofs, Tudor-type beams, and sometimes their latticed windows, though there were also Amersham flat-roofed sun houses, garages and even airports. The Amersham label is prominently displayed on the base. Amersham houses continued to be advertised in 1941 and, according to Marion Osborne, the firm continued making dollhouses after World War II. As she says, "There were different styles but it will be difficult to say definitely that a house is pre or post war. The best that can be said is that an Amersham house could be any time between 1930-*c*. 1957." Our example of an Amersham bungalow (below) falls into this category.

Needless to say, Germany was also mass-producing dollhouses during this period, and was exporting them all over the world with its customary skill. O. & M. Hausser, for example, was making its "Elastolin" houses "in perfect English style" in 1925, although to be honest, the example illustrated in its catalog does not look English at all. Its new cottages were described in 1927 as looking particularly attractive, being unbreakable and designed to represent a country cottage as realistically as possible.

The firm of D. H. Wagner exported its houses to England through the wholesaler Fred H. Allen, who set up his business in 1928. A year later, he was offering dollhouses with electric lights, and yet more country cottages. An advertisement in the *Toy Trader*, for January 1938, tells us that "D. H. Wagner & Sohn of Grunhainichen, in addition to the dolls' houses and forts that have been so successful in the past years, have produced two new 'English-style' dolls' houses for 1938," the accompanying drawing of which closely resembles photographs of those discovered by several collectors, which were first published in *International Dolls' House News* in black and white in 1988. The color photograph published in the same journal in 1994 shows a house with a steeply pitched, orange roof with darker patches of stenciled tiles, and brown timber beams on a cream ground. The windows were usually made of a mixture of cardboard and metal.

the firm of Hobbies is still in existence in Dereham, Norfolk, where it is owned by one of the 1930s designers of the firm and his family.

Another type of early twentieth-century dollhouse which has come to the fore recently through the pages of *International Dolls' House News* is the Amersham house. Produced in England in the late 1930s, these houses are distinguishable by their over-

That there was another major German manufacturer of dollhouses operating in the 1920s seems clear from entries in *Der Universaler Spielwaren Katalog* ["The Universal Toy Catalog"] for 1924-26, which shows an ornate white villa with balconies, beadlike balustrades, net curtains and a curiously

shaped red roof. This house does not resemble those of either Wagner or Gottschalk, but examples do appear in salesrooms from time to time, and there is a house of this type in the Musée des Arts Décoratifs in Paris, France.

As in the United States, plenty of large, handmade dollhouses were being produced in Europe in the first part of the twentieth century at the same time as these smaller domestic examples. The Spielzeugmuseum in Nuremberg has a fine wooden German house dated 1910, the Nordiska Museet in Stockholm has two early twentieth-century houses, and the Museovirasto, Helsinki, Finland, has a six-roomed cabinet house, dating from 1930, furnished in contemporary style. Doubtless there are dozens more scattered around museums throughout mainland Europe for, according to an article in *Games and Toys* magazine in 1926, Scandinavian toy stores made a speciality of dollhouses. The writer describes a large dollhouse, measuring eight by five feet, filled with the most perfect miniatures, and costing a mint of money.

In England, there are dollhouses like Devonshire Villas in the Bethnal Green Museum of Childhood in London; the Gandolfo house in the Precinct Toy Collection, Sandwich, Kent, made in 1908 and fully furnished in the style of that period; the 1914 house in the Lilliput Museum, Isle of Wight;

the Worthington house in the Warwick Doll and Toy Museum, made in 1916 for Helen Worthington, aged seven, by Lord Warwick's estate carpenter; and the 1920s Turner house

ABOVE:
A 1930s house by D. H. Wagner of Germany. This firm exported its dollhouses to England, producing "English-style" models in 1938. The steeply pitched roof painted with darker patches of stenciled tiles, and sometimes brown timber beams on a cream ground, are typical.

LEFT:
In complete contrast is this handmade dollhouse made in 1908. The Gandolfo house in the Precinct Toy Collection, Sandwich, Kent, is tall and built on three floors. Here you can see the dining room, filled with well-made wooden furniture, much of which came from Germany before World War I.

RIGHT:
The Worthington dollhouse was made for Helen Worthington, aged seven, by Lord Warwick's estate carpenter. Note the paneled entrance hall and dining room and the book-filled upstairs library.

BELOW:
The dollhouse at Michelham Priory, East Sussex, was made at about the same time as Queen Mary's dollhouse, and many of the items in it resemble those in that larger and more splendid house. This three-story house contains seven rooms and staircase halls. The kitchen and the nursery, crammed with toys, form a vivid re-creation of the 1920s.

at Michelham Priory, East Sussex, England. Another unique English dollhouse is "Mirror Grange," last seen at the Heritage Craft Schools for Crippled Children at Chailey, a charity for which it was first exhibited.

In England in the 1920s and 1930s there was a popular comic strip recounting the adventures of a trio of animals: a penguin, a dog, and a rabbit, named Pip, Squeak and Wilfred. A miniature house, named "Mirror

Grange," was designed for them by the architect Maxwell Ayrton, and it was accordingly built in 1929. This house, built on a wooden rocklike structure, became so famous that a book was even written about it. There were Pip, Squeak and Wilfred toys, and there was even a set of Pip, Squeak and Wilfred handkerchiefs with the animals printed on one corner, which was sold in a novelty box in the shape of a cottage. Each cottage had four

windows with mica panes, and one of the pets could be seen at each window. When the front door was opened, another version of one of the pets appeared – a clever form of early "spin-off" advertising.

In fact, the 1920s were a good period for dollhouses, for it was in this decade that two remarkable and now world-famous dollhouses were created in England: Titania's Palace, now at Legoland, Copenhagen, Denmark, and Queen Mary's dollhouse at Windsor Castle in England.

Titania's Palace was the brainchild of Sir Nevile Wilkinson, a soldier and an artist. In 1907 he was sketching a tree near his home in Ireland when his small daughter announced that she had seen a fairy disappearing into the roots of a nearby tree. Assuming that the fairy was Titania, queen of all fairies, he offered to build a palace for her and her husband, Oberon, a task which was to occupy a great deal of his time for the rest of his life.

The palace Wilkinson created is a large one, measuring nine by seven by two feet, built round a courtyard laid out as a garden, and designed to be seen from all four sides. The 18 halls and rooms are filled with more than 3000 small items, some of which are copies of real furniture, paintings and antiques, and it is hard to say which of the rooms, many of which were decorated by Sir Nevile himself, is the most splendid of all.

The four state apartments are certainly very spectacular. They comprise the "Hall of the Fairy Kiss," the chapel, the "Hall of the Guilds," and the throne room, and all are sumptuously decorated with miniature inlay, mosaic, marble, painting and ornaments. The Hall of the Fairy Kiss, the formal entrance hall to the palace, has a minstrel gallery ornamented with silver and bronze figures, a glass casket containing the "Insignia of the Fairy Kiss," and silver grilles designed to keep junior fairies from flying in. The mosaic windows in the chapel are made of translucent enamel, and the organ can actually be played, albeit only with a match. The Hall of the Guilds, with its miniature mechanical fountain set with diamonds, leads to the throne room, which has a peacock throne made out of a brooch believed to have belonged to the Empress Eugénie of France. It is ornamented with diamonds, rubies and sapphires. In the center of the room is Titania's pearl-studded royal crown.

Titania's Palace was nearing completion when Sir Nevile heard rumors of the work being done on Queen Mary's dollhouse. He wanted to complete his work of art before this rival dollhouse could be seen by the public, but there was still a great deal to achieve. In the end, he did exhibit it in 1922, before Queen Mary's house, but only by showing it unfinished.

Queen Mary's dollhouse was the idea of a cousin of King George V, Princess Marie Louise, a childhood friend of Queen Mary. The famous architect Sir Edwin Lutyens was commissioned to design it, and it was he who sought out and co-ordinated the ideas of nearly 1500 tradesmen, artists and authors. The house was paid for by private gifts and donations. The queen herself took a great interest in its construction and furnishing, as indeed she would, since she was a lifelong collector of antiques and miniatures. After four years of intensive work, the dollhouse was exhibited for the first time at the Wembley Exhibition in 1924.

Just as Princess Augusta Dorothea's rooms at Arnstadt show the court life of the eighteenth century, Queen Mary's mansion depicts a court residence of the twentieth century, forming a unique record of life at that time in a royal household.

Nearly everything in it was especially commissioned (unlike Titania's Palace, in which some of the items were secondhand) and, such is the perfection of the craftsmanship, that when looking at the rooms it is difficult to realize that we are not looking at a full-sized house. The 40 rooms and vestibules in the house include a magnificent library filled with books commissioned from authors living at that time, a dining room, the king's suite and the queen's suite, each with its own private bathroom with running water, a day and a night nursery, a playroom, an elegant salon, and many other rooms which are described and photographed in great detail in Mary Stewart-Wilson's fascinating book, *Queen Mary's Dolls' House* (published by Bodley Head in 1988).

The finishing touch to this magnificent house is provided by the garden, planned by Gertrude Jekyll, the renowned landscape gardener, which is contained in a drawer, the trees lying flat when the drawer is closed. In it, roses climb over the back wall, a ring of toadstools grows on a path, a snail winds its way along a row of bricks, and a thrush sits on a nest of eggs.

Chapter V
Late Twentieth-Century Dollhouses in Europe and the U.S.A.

Although craftsmen have continued to use wood for their dollhouses, the manufactured dollhouses of the latter half of the twentieth century have been characterized by their innovative use of different materials such as various types of board, tin, and plastic and, more recently, wood-and-plastic.

The firm of Louis Marx in the U.S.A. had considerable success with its tin houses and furniture in the years following World War II. Louis Marx was born in New York in 1884, working at an early age for a manufacturer of clockwork toys. In 1921 he started his own business with his brother, making tin toys of all kinds, including dollhouses and later on, good-quality plastic dollhouse furniture in classic styles. He was immensely successful – a millionaire before he was 30 years old – owning six factories in the U.S.A. and more in other parts of the world, until the firm ceased trading in the early 1970s.

According to Mary Harris, a Canadian collector writing in the summer 1988 issue of *International Dolls' House News*, the early Marx dollhouses dating from the late 1940s had nonopening tin doors and tin windows, while by the 1950s and 1960s the firm was using plastic for doors and windows. Later still, the chimneys, roofs and the tabs holding the house together were also made of plastic, but some of the windows had reverted to tin. She shows a photograph of an unusual trademark of 1974 on possibly one of the last Marx dollhouses to be made, which states that the firm was by then "a subsidiary of the Quaker Oats Company."

The scale of the larger houses was three-quarters of an inch to a foot, but the smaller bungalows were only half an inch to the foot. They were exported packed flat, with the plastic furniture for each room neatly parceled in labeled paper bags.

At about the same time in England, the firm of Mettoy was also making tin dollhouses

OPPOSITE PAGE, TOP:
A Louis Marx metal dollhouse, c.1950. This picture shows how the dollhouses were exported from America packed flat, with their furniture neatly parceled in labeled paper bags.

OPPOSITE PAGE, BOTTOM:
A Louis Marx metal bungalow. These bungalows were on a smaller scale than the houses, at half an inch to a foot.

BELOW:
An attractively designed English Mettoy metal house, with a plastic chimney and front door.

BELOW:
A Chad Valley metal suburban villa of about 1963. This firm started as a printing works but expanded into toys, then into metal boxes and, by natural progression, into metal toys.

with plastic chimneys and front doors in attractive designs, as was the long-established firm of Chad Valley, primarily famous for its soft toys but also a manufacturer of lithographed tin toys, including dollhouses.

The firm of Hobbies continued to publish designs for dollhouses for D.I.Y. enthusiasts up until the late 1960s, when it went out of business for a while. The popular Tudor-type design of the 1930s was changed after the war

to bring it more up to date by giving it metal latticed windows and metal doors, doing away with the two bay windows and having only one gable. The roof also changed, to one covered with tile-effect paper, while the little garage altered its shape from lean-to to doghouse. Hobbies still produce *The Hobbies Handbook, The Toy and Model Making Annual*, which includes ideas for making dollhouses and other toys. This is not to be confused with *Hobby's*

Annual, in which dollhouse kits are shown ranging from American late Victorian with gingerbread trim to "snap-together" Storybook cottages in the 1:12 scale.

The firm of Tri-ang was not idle during the postwar years, as can be seen in Marion Osborne's book *Lines and Tri-ang Dolls' Houses and Furniture, 1900-1971*. The firm produced a large range of houses of all types, reflecting the changes in domestic architecture over the decades. The small, modern, Tudor-influenced house appears in the 1939 catalog alongside a "suntrap" house with a penthouse sun room and a six-roomed mansion suitable for a wealthy stockbroker tired of the usual Tudor. By 1950, the "Queen Anne" house had arrived, and by 1957 a typical 1950s stone-fronted house with an up-and-over

garage door and plastic windows. Interestingly, by 1963 Tri-ang had also produced a metal-fronted house, a seven-roomed modern bungalow with sunshine windows, a pack-flat house, and "Jenny's Home," a modular series of plastic rooms; but the small 1939 Tudor cottage remained unchanged and unchallenged in the catalog. By 1971, plastic roofs, windows and shutters on the dollhouses were marking the end of an era.

In 1945, after World War II, the firm of Barton set up in south London, making dollhouse furniture. Ten years later it moved farther south to the suburb of New Addington, where it produced a flat-pack dollhouse in typical 1950s style (called "Addington Lodge") in lightweight wood. It was designed to be fitted out with Barton's up-to-date furniture, which

ABOVE:
The English firm of Hobbies specialized in dollhouse designs for D.I.Y. enthusiasts. This 1951 house was built from a Hobbies pattern, the Tudor-type façade of an earlier date brought up-to-the-minute by means of metal windows and doors and the changed garage shape.

ABOVE:
An overview of the interior of the 1951 Hobbies dollhouse. The inside is uncomplicated, with the staircase halls on the left. The four rooms are well proportioned and there is extra space in the front bays.

RIGHT:
The Tri-ang 1957/58 house, with an up-and-over garage door and plastic windows.

included things like T.V. sets and modern kitchens equipped with cutlery boxes and plastic cups and saucers. More information about the products of the firm of Barton, and particularly about its range of dollhouse furniture, can be found in Marion Osborne's book *Barton's "Model Homes."*

By the early 1970s, the Swedish firm of Lundby was increasing its share of the market and, to combat this, by 1976 Barton had produced an even more up-to-date dollhouse named "Caroline's Home," with its own set of brightly colored plastic furniture, followed in 1980 by a "Super de Luxe Caroline's Home." A few years later Barton was taken over by Lundby and was still making Caroline's Home in the U.K. in 1987. The U.K. subsidiary of

Lundby disappeared recently, but the firm of Lundby still makes and exports its good-quality dollhouses from Sweden. One of the latest catalogs shows a picture of the "Goteborg" house, which is much in the style of the well-loved Caroline's Home.

Also from Scandinavia, Hanse of Denmark was exporting its open-plan card and plastic dollhouses to Europe in the 1970s, which could be filled with the firm's own furniture, known as "Princess Veronique," or with that of Lundby or Barton.

By this time the use of plastic was fairly commonplace, and there were several all-plastic dollhouses on the market. The Hong Kong "Blue Box" houses exported to Europe in the 1970s are a good example of the small,

ABOVE:
The small, Tudor-type Tri-ang dollhouse which appeared in the catalog from 1939 until 1963. Its popularity probably had a lot to do with its handy size: 17 inches long and 14 inches wide.

BELOW:
The Swedish firm of Lundby was exporting to the rest of Europe in quantity by the 1970s, its modern, wooden houses having a great influence on other dollhouse designs. The clean lines and open plan of this house are a complete change from previous dollhouses.

RIGHT:
To combat the dominance of Lundby, Barton produced "Caroline's Home" in 1976. This too was an up-to-date open-plan house, with plastic windows, doors and furniture.

BELOW:
Another Scandinavian firm, Hanse of Denmark, was also exporting its card and plastic open-plan dollhouses in the 1970s.

OPPOSITE PAGE, TOP:
An all-plastic 1970s open-plan dollhouse by the Hong Kong firm of Blue Box. This was in 1:16 scale and had its own range of plastic furniture.

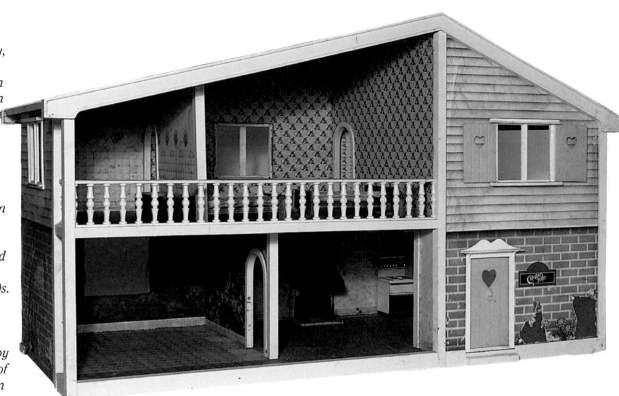

inexpensive, all-plastic house which could be equipped with pieces of plastic furniture designed on the same diminutive scale. The firm of Blue Box celebrated its fortieth anniversary in 1991, and is still producing its large range of toys in Hong Kong, China, Singapore and Malaysia for export.

The American firm of Fisher-Price began to experiment with plastic for its toys in the 1950s, and by the mid-1960s the use of this material had transformed its designs, allowing more innovation, brighter colors that did not fade, and safe toys of high quality. The Fisher-Price style is very distinctive, based as it is on research into what children like at each age and into safety and durability factors, all backed by an insistence that learning should be a pleasurable activity.

The Fisher-Price dollhouse, a two-story building with access to rooms at the front and back, embodies this thinking. It folds up so that it can be carried (along with its sturdy plastic contents) from room to room, and it has doors that open and a doorbell that rings. That the colors seem sugary and unrealistic is an adult judgment, and is neither here nor there for the thousands of small girls (from three years old and up) who are delighted to own such a dollhouse.

Recent arrivals on the plastic dollhouse

scene include homes for a group of small, fluffy animals of great charm, known as the Sylvanian family (made by Tomy). Since they were launched in 1987 they have collectively been toy of the year for three years. They were

BELOW:
The Victorian-style 1993 Fisher-Price all-plastic dollhouse.

given a beautifully crafted windmill to live in in 1990, a country mansion a little later, and they also have a smart canal boat with all its accessories. Marion Osborne writes of

a sewing machine complete with three reels of cotton, a pin cushion, scissors and a metre ruler. Wardrobes have coat hangers, bookshelves have books and the tiny dollhouse has furniture. The school items include tambourine, recorder, tubes of paints etc., all in the correct scale and most desirable for those who like the little things in life.

Another firm making plastic dollhouses is Playmobil (U.K.), which in 1990 launched a pretty turn-of-the-century playhouse with five rooms, a terrace, a balcony and summer lounge on the first and second floors, and an attic. The whole interior is ready-wallpapered, decorated with mirrors and movable pictures, drapes, carpets and flower boxes and a complete family in period costume. Accessories include furniture, a street photographer with camera and tripod, a horse-drawn delivery cart, and a delivery van.

Bodo Hennig is a German firm that makes use of both wood and plastic in its high-class dollhouse rooms and furniture and, as might be expected, Mattel's Barbie doll and her companion Ken now have a plastic dollhouse with

patio, that folds neatly away into a carrying box when play is finished.

There have been paper and cardboard houses for the past century, so the many dollhouses in book form that can be purchased today are following an established tradition. In 1983 Purnell published *Make a Model Victorian House* for British retailers Marks and Spencer, and 10 years later Usborne Publishing Ltd. produced a model house in Victorian style. Both are good examples of their kind, with their clear instructions and fine detailing. Particularly endearing is the way in which the cutout pieces are printed on the back as well as the front, so that when you have a figure sitting on a chair, you can turn it round and get the back view of the same figure. Simon and Schuster publish *The Doll's House Carousel*, which is reminiscent of the McLoughlin Dolly's Playhouse, and there is even a cutout book version of Sara Ploos van Amstel's second dollhouse in Haarlem, based on the real thing. This is published by Uitgeverij Thoth, and a watercolor has been made for it of each wall of the 12 rooms of the dollhouse. The publication is accompanied by an introduction on the history and design of the house.

Alongside the plastic and paper dollhouses, many good-quality wooden houses in kit form

OPPOSITE PAGE:
Recent arrivals on the plastic dollhouse scene include homes for a charming family of animals knowns as the Sylvanians. Since they were launched by Tomy in 1987 they have collectively been toy of the year for three years. This windmill was given to them to live in in 1990.

BELOW:
Many dollhouses in book form can be purchased today. In 1993 Usborne Publishing Ltd. produced its model paper house in Victorian style. Its clear instructions and fine detailing would give pleasure to a practical child who likes to make things.

OPPOSITE PAGE:
*An Emmerson Row
wooden kit dollhouse by
Greenleaf.*

BELOW:
*A dollhouse made from
a D.I.Y. kit by
Honeychurch.*

or ready-made in a variety of designs have been produced for reasonable prices in recent years in the U.K. by firms such as Honeychurch and Dolphin, and by Greenleaf of the U.S.A., which exports to Europe. Honeychurch also produces an attractive range of wooden furniture to go in its houses, made from Canadian maple.

Meanwhile, fine craftsmen like Kevin Mulvaney and Susan Rogers of the U.K., Jim Marcus of the U.S.A., and many others, have continued to make dollhouses that match and often surpass in quality those of the past. Kevin Mulvaney and Susan Rogers' most famous constructions are the amazingly detailed, six-and-a-half-foot-high model of

BELOW:
The magnificent "Versailles," by Kevin Mulvaney and Susan Rogers. This amazingly detailed model is six-and-a-half feet high.

OPPOSITE PAGE, TOP:
The German firm of Bodo Hennig has recently produced two delightful miniature kitchens. The modern kitchen is a typical 1990s room.

OPPOSITE PAGE, BOTTOM:
The cosy-looking Bodo Hennig old-style kitchen is full of domestic detail, from the metal stove to the cooking implements on the rack at the back of the room.

LEFT:
This McAllister Street house, San Francisco, was built by Jim Marcus of Alameda in 1975. One of a series of five, it is made to be free-standing or wall hung.

BELOW:
The interior of the McAllister Street house made by Jim Marcus in 1975, consisting of three rooms.

RIGHT:
"The Palace," made by Evaline Ness in the 1970s. The dollhouse is noted for its needlework tapestries.

RIGHT, BELOW:
Kingscote house. Built in 1987 by Norm Nielsen, Sr., and designed by Richard Upjohn.

BELOW:
*The Beach House, made
c.1919, which can now
be viewed at Angels
Attic in Santa Monica,
California.*

PAGE 80:
*This fine dollhouse
dates from the
nineteenth century, and
was probably made by
Gottschalk.*

Versailles, finished in 1992 and now in Angels Attic, California, and the later Château de Fontainebleau, also a large model with finely decorated interiors, housed in a museum in the U.S.A. Their Albert Hall, finished in 1993, is in a private museum in London.

Jim Marcus is famous for his meticulous copies of the façades of San Francisco's Victorian houses, one of which, shown here, was made in 1975 as one of a series of five, intended to be freestanding or wall hung. This dollhouse is one of the many to be seen at Angels Attic, California, among them a fine

Southern colonial mansion of eight rooms, designed and built in 1969 by the late Susie Hendrix. Angels Attic is a nonprofitmaking enterprise for the benefit of a center which is dedicated to the education and treatment of autistic children and young adults and those with learning difficulties.

The Museum of the City of New York also has a fine handmade dollhouse named "The Palace," made in the 1970s by the late Evaline Ness (see Chapter III for details), whose husband, Arnold A. Bayard, donated it to the museum in memory of his wife.

Bibliography

Earnshaw, Nora. *Collecting Dolls' Houses and Miniatures*, Collins, London, 1989.

Eaton, Faith. *The Miniature House*, Weidenfeld and Nicolson Ltd., London, 1990.

Greene, Vivien. *English Dolls' Houses of the Eighteenth and Nineteenth Centuries*, B.T. Batsford Ltd., London, 1955 (reissued 1979).

Greene, Vivien. *Family Dolls' Houses*, G. Bell & Sons, London, 1973.

International Dolls' House News, 1984-94.

Jackson, Valerie. *Dolls' Houses and Miniatures*, John Murray (Publishers) Ltd., London, 1988.

Jacobs, Flora Gill. *Dolls' Houses in America*, Charles Scribner's Sons, New York, 1974.

King, Constance Eileen. *The Collector's History of Dolls' Houses*, Robert Hale Ltd., London, 1983.

Leber, Wolfgang. "*Die Puppenstadt* Mon Plaisir" ["The Dolls' Town of *Mon Plaisir*"], *Veröffentlichungen der Museen der Stadt Arnstadt* [Publications of the Museums of the Town of Arnstadt], Arnstadt, 1986.

Manos, Susan. *Schoenhut Dolls & Toys*, Collector Books, Kentucky, 1976.

Osborne, Marion. *A to Z, 1914 to 1941, Dolls' Houses*.

Osborne, Marion. *Barton's "Model Homes"*.

Osborne, Marion. *Lines and Tri-ang Dolls' Houses and Furniture*, 1900-1971.

Pijzel-Dommisse, Jet. "*Het Poppenhuis van het Haags Gemeentemuseum*" ["The Dolls' House of the Haags Gemeentemuseum"], The Hague, 1988.

Stewart-Wilson, Mary. *Queen Mary's Dolls' House*, Bodley Head, London, 1988.

Towner, Margaret. *Dolls' House Furniture*, Apple Press, London, 1993.

Whitton, Blair (ed.). *Bliss Toys and Doll Houses*, Dover Publications Inc., New York, in association with The Margaret Woodbury Strong Museum, 1979.

Wilckens, Leoni von. *The Dolls' House*, Bell & Hyman Ltd., London, 1980.

Acknowledgments

The author would particularly like to thank the following: Nick Nicholson, photographer; Graham and Jackie Munday, the Lilliput Museum, Isle of Wight; Nick and Esther Forder, *International Dolls' House News*; Ann and Stan Colby, Burwash Weald; Mrs. Barbara Andrews; and Flora Gill Jacobs, the Washington Dolls' House and Toy Museum. The publisher would like to thank Ron Callow of D23 for designing this book; Clare Haworth-Maden, editor; Suzanne O'Farrell and Sara Dunphy for the picture research; and Simon Shelmerdine for production. The following individuals and agencies provided photographic material:

Mrs. Barbara Andrews/Photo, Nick Nicholson: pages 35, 36(top)

Courtesy Angels Attic, Santa Monica, CA: page 45(top)/On loan from the collection of Jackie McMahan: pages 75, 76, 78

Arnstadt Castle Museum, Germany/Photo, Nick Nicholson: pages 7, 22(both)

Reproduced by permission of the Marquess of Bath, Longleat House, Warminster, Wiltshire, Great Britain/Photo, Lord Christopher Thynne: page 19

The Bridgeman Art Library/Bethnal Green Museum, London: page 36(bottom)

Buckley's Yesterday World, Battle, Surrey/Photo, Nick Nicholson: page 50

Captain and Mrs. Bulwer Long/Photo, Nick Nicholson: page 14(both)

Cockthorpe Hall Museum of Childhood, Norfolk/Photo, Nick Nicholson: page 39(bottom)

Ann and Stan Colby, Burwash Weald/Photo, Nick Nicholson: pages 52(bottom), 58(bottom), 60, 61, 62(both), 63, 66(both), 67(top)

Collection of the Denver Museum of Miniatures, Dolls and Toys, CO. Gift to the museum by Mr. and Mrs. Alfred O'Meara, Jr.: page 77(bottom)

The Dolls' House, Bromley, Kent/Photo, Nick Nicholson: page 71

Farnham Museum, Surrey, on loan from private collection/Photo, Nick Nicholson: page 15

Fisher-Price, Berkshire: page 67(bottom)

Mrs. Lorna Gandolfo (The Precinct Toy Collection, Sandwich, Kent)/Photo, Nick Nicholson: pages 53(bottom), 60

Germanisches Nationalmuseum, Nuremberg, Germany/Photo, Nick Nicholson: pages 8, 9, 10, 11(both)

Haags Gemeentemuseum, The Hague, The Netherlands/Photo, Nick Nicholson: pages 3, 20(both)

Frans Halsmuseum, Haarlem, The Netherlands: page 21

Rutherford B. Hayes Presidential Center/Gilbert Gonzalez, Fremont, OH: page 1

Courtesy Historical Society of Delaware, Wilmington, DE: page 42(top)

Historisches Museum, Basel, Switzerland/Photo, Maurice Babey: page 30

Honeychurch, Wiltshire, England, at the Dorking Dolls' House Gallery, Surrey/Photo, Nick Nicholson: page 70

International Dolls' House News/Photo, Nick Nicholson: pages 53(top), 58(top), 59, 68, 74-75(both)

The Trustees of the Edward James Foundation, West Dean, Sussex/Photo, Nick Nicholson: pages 12, 13

King's Lynn Social History Museum/Photo, Nick Nicholson: page 18(both)

Legoland, Denmark: pages 30(top), 57(top)

Lilliput Museum, Isle of Wight/Photo, Nick Nicholson: pages 34(bottom), 51(bottom), 52(top)

Michelham Priory, Sussex/Photo, Nick Nicholson: page 54(bottom)

Milwaukee Public Museum, Milwaukee, WI: page 24(bottom)

Kevin Mulvaney and Susan Rogers, London: pages 72-73

Musée des Arts Décoratifs, Paris/Photo, Nick Nicholson: pages 6, 28, 80

Musée des Arts Populaires, Paris/Photo, Nick Nicholson: page 29

Museum of American History, Smithsonian Institution, Washington, D.C.: page 42(bottom)

Museum of the City of New York/Gift of Mr. John W. G. Tenney and Philip Milledoler Brett, Jr. (acc. no. 61.235): page 25(top)/Gift of Captain Marion Eppley (acc. no. 54.5.12): page 25(bottom)/Made by Miss Carrie Stettheimer, Gift of Miss Ettie Stettheimer (acc. no. 45.121.1), photo by Lynton Gardiner: page 48(bottom)/Made by Evaline Ness, Gift of Arnold A. Bayard, in memory of his wife, Evaline Ness (acc. no. 87.72), photo by Helga Studio: pages 76-77(top)

Museum of London: page 33

Museum of Science and Industry, Chicago, IL/Photo, Nick Nicholson: page 49(both)

The National Board of Antiquities, The National Museum of Finland: page 32(bottom)

Nationalmuseet Copenhagen, Denmark, Niels Elswing: pages 23(bottom), 31(bottom), 32(top)

© The National Trust/Photo, Nick Nicholson: pages 4-5, 16(both), 17(top), 37, 38, 39(top)

Nick Nicholson, 3 Weston Close, Ballfield Road, Godalming, Surrey GU7 2EY: pages 26, 34(top), 44(bottom), 50, 51(top), 55

Nordiska Museet, Stockholm/Photo, Birgit Brånvall: pages 23(top), 64-65

Courtesy Peabody and Essex Museum, Salem, MA: page 40

The Royal Collection, © 1994, Her Majesty the Queen: page 57(bottom)

Courtesy The Strong Museum, Rochester, NY, © 1994: page 45(bottom)

Toy and Miniature Museum, Kansas City, MO: page 41

Usborne Publishing, London, in: *Make This Model Doll's House*: page 69

Vestlandske Kunstindustrimuseum, Bergen, Norway/Photo, Egil Korsnes: page 24(top)

Warwick Doll and Toy Museum/Photo, Nick Nicholson: page 54(top)

Washington Dolls' House & Toy Museum, Washington, D.C.: pages 43(top), 44(top), 46(both), 48(top)

Courtesy of the Wenham Museum, Wenham, MA: page 43(left)

York Castle Museum: page 17(bottom)